THE ADVENTURES OF THE GOOROO NOODLE

THE ADVENTURES OF THE GOOROO NOODLE

A TALE IN THE TAMIL LANGUAGE

TRANSLATED BY
BENJAMIN BABINGTON

GYAN

Published by

Gyan Publishing House
5, Ansari Road
Daryaganj, New Delhi-110002
Phone: 011-47034999, 9811692060
E-mail: books@gyanbooks.com

Distribution Network
gyanbooks.com
India, USA, Canada, UK, Australia, France

ISBN : 978-81-212-3097-1 (PB)
First Published, 1915

2nd Impression 2020

Printed at: Gyan Press, Delhi.

The Adventures of the Gooroo Noodle
Author: Benjamin Babington

THE ADVENTURES

OF THE

GOOROO NOODLE

A TALE IN THE TAMIL LANGUAGE

TRANSLATED BY

BENJAMIN BABINGTON

OF THE MADRAS CIVIL SERVICE

REPRINTED AND PUBLISHED BY

PANINI OFFICE, BAHADURGANJ, ALLAHABAD

1915

CONTENTS.

FOREWORD BY THE TRANSLATOR.

The Story of the Gooroo Paramârtan is one of the lighter productions of that profound scholar and rare genius, father Beschi. Vîramâmooni or the great Champion Devotee, as Beschi is surnamed by the Tamils, was a native of Italy, and one of the religious order of Jesuits. Having been appointed by the Pope to the East India Mission, he arrived, in 1700, at the city of Goa, on the Western coast. He thence proceeded to Âvoor, in the district of Trichinopoly, where he studied the Tamil language in both its dialects, as well as the Sanskrit and Teloogoo ; and with a view to public employment, which it was ever the Jesuit policy to seek in order to promote their religious views, he made himself master of the Hindostanee and Persian. It is probable that he held political offices in the earlier part of his life, for we can hardly suppose him to have risen at once to the appointment of Divan, which he held under the celebrated Chunda Saheb, during his rule as Nabob of Trichinopoly, especially as Chunda Sahib did not assume the government of that place until the death of the Rajah, which happened in the year 1736.

From the moment of his arrival in India, he, in conformity with Hindoo custom, abandoned the use of animal food, and employed Brahmans to prepare his meals. He adopted the habit of a religious devotee, and on his visitations to his flock assumed all the pomp and pageantry with which Hindoo Gooroos usually travel. He founded a church at Konângooppam Ariyanoor, in the district of Baroor, and my MS. notices particularly a picture of the Madonna and the child Jesus, which he caused to be painted at

Manilla and set up in that church. It was in honour of this Madonna, of her husband Joseph and the Lord Jesus, that he composed the Sacred Poem called Têmbâvani : which, vying in length with the Iliad itself, is by far the most voluminous of his works. It contains 3,615 tetrastichs, each of which is furnished with a prose interpretation ; and, to judge from the only Padalam or Canto which I have had an opportunity of reading, where the murder of the innocents is described, its merits are not over-rated. Vîramâmooni also founded a church at Tirookâvaloor, a name which he gave to the town of Vadoogapet, in the district of Ariyaloor, and on the Madonna there he composed three Poems: Tirookâvaloor Kalambagam, Anneiyajoongal Andâdi, and Adeikala Mâlei.—The following are the most important of the remaining works of this author; which, with exceptions that will be noticed, are extant only in MS.

Kitêri Ammâl Ammânei, a poem. Vêdiyarojookkam, a work in prose; where, as the name implies, the duties of one who has devoted his life to religion are laid down. Vêda Vilakkam, also in prose; which, from the title (the light of the gospel), I presume to contain some doctrinal exposition of the Roman

Catholic Faith. A Dictionary, Tamil and French; another Tamil and Portuguese; a third Tamil and Latin. Sadoor Agharâdi, or the Four Dictionaries; a Tamil work relating to the higher dialect. Of philological works he has furnished Tonnool Vilakkam; a Tamil Grammar of the higher dialect, written in Latin. Of this I made a Translation in 1814; which, having become the property of the Madras Government, is now, as I learn, under course of publication at their College Press. The Clavis Humaniorum Tamulici Idiomatis; a second Grammatical Treatise in Latin, relating to the higher dialect. A Latin Grammar of the common dialect ; which has been published at the College Press at Madras ; and of which a faulty and vulgar translation has long been before the public.

Such were the literary labours of Beschi, and he was distinguished as much for his piety and benevolence as for his learning. Vîramâmooni continued to hold the office of Divan, in Trichinopoly, until the year 1740 ; when that city being besieged by the Mahrattha army, under Morary Rao, and Chunda Saheb being taken prisoner, he contrived to effect his escape, and fled to the city of Gâyal Patanam, then belonging to the Dutch. He there remained, in the service of the church, until 1742, when he was carried off by an illness, the particulars of which are not stated. His name is still remembered in Gâyal Patanam, and masses continue to be offered up for the salvation of his soul, in that city and its neighbourhood.

THE ADVENTURES OF THE GOOROO NOODLE

FIRST STORY

OF THE PASSAGE OVER THE RIVER

THERE was a Gooroo* whose name was Noodle, who had five

* For an account of the office and powers of the Gooroo, the reader is referred to the Abbé Dubois' work, on the Manners and Customs, &c. of the Hindoos. He will also be enabled to judge of the reverence paid this sacred character by a reference to the Institutes of Manu, Ch. xi., verses 229, 230 and 232.

disciples serving under his command, Blockhead, Idiot, Simpleton, Dunce and Fool. These, having all six gone on foot through the surrounding villages, to make some enquiries respecting other disciples, were on their return to their Matham,* when one day, they arrived in the third watch, at the bank of a river.

Under a notion that this was a cruel stream, which in consequence, could not be passed while it was awake, the Gooroo gave orders to Dunce, and dispatched him to

---

* The Matham is a secluded retreat, in which the Gooroo and his disciples reside when not engaged in visitations to those who are under their spiritual control.

ascertain whether the river were asleep. Upon this he lighted with a cigar, and carried with him, a firebrand* which he had borne in his hand, and without approaching the river, kept aloof and stretching out the brand at arm's length, dipped it into the water.

Observing that as soon as he had immersed it, the water smoked with a hissing noise, away Dunce ran, hurrying, stumbling and tumbling, and cried out, "O Master!

---

* The firebrands used in India are either large stakes of a kind of wood (ixora parviflora) containing bitumen enough to support a flame, and which are analogous to the *tedæ* of the Ancients, or they are, as described by Tavernier, "un linge entortillé et trempé dans l' huile que l'on met dans une maniere de rechaut au bout d'un baton."

Master ! this is not the time for passing the river. It is awake ; and no sooner had I touched it, than it flew into a passion, hissed like a venomous serpent, and smoking in fierce rage, leaped and rushed at me. It is indeed a wonder that I escaped with my life." To this the Gooroo replied, "What can we do in opposition to the divine will ? We will wait a little while." So saying, they sat down in a spreading grove hard by, which formed a dark shade, and as each was relating, in order to pass the time there, different circumstances regarding this river, Blockhead spoke as follows :

" I have many a time heard my Grandfather tell of the ferocity and artfulness of this stream. My Grandfather was a great merchant. One day, he and a companion of his were driving along two asses laden with bags of salt, and when they had descended into the middle of the river, they washed them selves in the cool water, which was running up to their waists, (for, as it was in the hot season, they were somewhat fatigued) and stopping the asses they bathed them also.

" On arriving afterwards at the opposite bank, they saw, not only that the river had devoured the whole of the salt, but that the salt had all been miraculously drawn out, while the mouths of the gunny bags, which were well sewed, were not in the least opened. They congratulated themselves, saying, ha! ha! since the river has seized upon this salt, is it not a great blessing that it has left us unswallowed?"

Upon this Simpleton began another anecdote. "The stratagems, wiles and thefts of this river have been numerous even in my day. Listen to one. A dog* holding fast in his mouth a piece of mutton

* The reader will here recognize a fable with which he is familiar. The author has more than once, as will presently be seen, introduced current stories which seemed to suit his purpose.

which he had stolen, was swimming in the middle of the stream, when the river deceitfully exhibited in its water another piece of flesh. As for the dog, he conceived, that, without any deceit, what he saw was the bigger; so, when quitting the piece which he held, he dived to snap at the larger one, both the one and the other disappeared, and the dog went home empty."

Whilst they were thus discoursing, they spied a horseman coming from the other side. As only a single span depth of water was flowing in the river, he remained on horseback, and without being the least afraid, came hastily splashing through. On perceiving this, they cried out, "Alack! alack! if our Gooroo too had a horse, both he and we with him might descend into the river without fear." Then they began to entreat him, saying, "O Sir, you must by all means buy a horse." The Gooroo Noodle, however, replied, "we will talk of this matter hereafter."

So as the day was declining and the evening approached, he sent again to examine whether the river were asleep. Idiot accordingly took the same fire-brand, and on immersing it for the purpose of examination, he found that the water did not spirt up in the least, as the fire had been before extinguished ; so being greatly delighted, he ran off, crying, "Now is the time ! now is the time ; come along quickly, and do not open your mouths or make any noise ; the time of the deep slumber of the river is come ; there is no occasion now for fear or alarm." Upon Idiot's shouting out this good news, they suddenly started up, and without uttering a single word, all six of them cautiously descended into the stream. At each step, which was so planted that even the waves beaten up by their legs made no rippling sound, they raised their feet over the water, advanced them, pressed them down again, and with hearts beating pit-a-pat tripped along and passed the river.

As soon as they reached and ascended the bank, they were elated in proportion as they had before been sorrowful, and while they were jumping about, Fool, who stood behind, counted all the rest without including himself.* As he only

---

* This story bears so close a resemblance to the 10th of "the merry Tales of the Wise Men of Gotham,' that we cannot but conclude, either that it was' borrowed from that Tale, or what is more probable, that both had their origin in some commonly current story. The Merry Tales to which I allude are now so scarce, that the reader will perhaps have no opportunity of determining this important point unless assisted by the following extract :

"On a certain time there were twelve men of Gotham that went to fish, and some stood on dry land ; and in going home one said to the other, We have ventured wonderfully in wading, I pray God that none of us come home to be drowned. Nay, marry, said one to the other, let us see that, for there did

saw five persons while he was counting, he took alarm, crying out, " Woe is me ! woe is me ! one is gone with the stream. Behold, Master, but five of us stand here." Having placed them all in a row, the

---

twelve of us come out. Then they told themselves, and every one told eleven ; said the one to the other, there is one of us drowned. They went back to the brook where they had been fishing, and sought up and down for him that was wanting, making great lamentation. A courtier coming by, asked what it was they sought for, and why they were sorrowful. O! said they, this day we went to fish in the brook; twelve of us come out together, and one is drowned. Said the courtier, tell how many there be of you ; one of them said eleven, and he did not tell himself. Well, said the courtier, what will you give me, and I will find the twelfth man. Sir, said they, all the money we have got. Give me the money, said the courtier, and began with the first, and gave him a stroke over the shoulders with his whip, which made him groan, saying, here is one : and so served them all, and they all groaned at the matter. When he came to the last, he paid him well, saying, here is the twelfth man. God's blessing on thy heart, said they, for thus finding our dear brother."

Gooroo himself counted them two or three times over; but as he always reckoned, omitting himself, he too pronounced that there were but five. Thus as one and all, each leaving himself out, added together only the others, it became certain among them that the river had swallowed up one.

On this account they howled bitterly, crying out " Alas! alas!" and embracing one another exclaimed, " O thou cruel river. O thou more obdurate than a block, more savage than a panther. Hast thou not feared, yea but a little, to swallow up the disciple of the Gooroo Noodle, who is saluted, respected, worshipped and praised from one end of the world to the other? Wretch! hast thou such a daring spirit, thou son of a black bear; offspring of a cruel tiger! Shalt thou attain to a future world? Shalt thou hereafter roll thy cool stream along? May thy source be totally dried up and scorched; may the glare dart upon the sand in thy bed; may fire feed upon thy waves; may thy belly be parched and withered; may thy depths be filled with thorns! Without moisture, without coolness, without even a mark to point out the place of thy former existence, mayest thou be in future consumed away!"

Thus did they vent their abuse and railing, stretching forth their hands and cracking their fingers.* Nevertheless, from their hasty stupidity, no one knew up to that moment which among them had been carried away by the river, and no one enquired who it might be. Just at that juncture, a sensible man who was travelling along the road came up and touched with compassion demanded, "How now Master, how now, tell me, what is this bustle about?" They in turn

---

* The Hindoos in uttering a malediction, unite their hands by interlacing the fingers, and then projecting them forwards produce that sound commonly called cracking the joints. Their imprecations are still further strengthened, as they think, by casting dust at the object of them.

related to him in due order what had happened, and he fully perceiving their idiotism replied, " What has happened, has happened.* If you will make me a suitable recompense, I have power to call hither him who is gone with the stream ; for know, that I am deeply versed in legerdemain." To that the Gooroo rejoicing answered, " If you will do this, we will give you forty-five fanams which we have provided for our journey." Then the other raising a stick which he held in his hand, " 'Tis in this," said he, " that this art is contained. If you will range yourselves in a row, and as

* That is, what has taken place is irremediable.

you receive a blow upon the back, will each reckon by calling out his name, I will cause all six of you to be here present." Having thus placed them, he first gave the Gooroo a thump on the back: "Holla!" cried he, "'tis I, myself, the Gooroo." "One," replied the man. In this manner he gave a blow to all of them, and each repeating his name respectively and casting up the account, they agreed in finding that not one among the six was missing. Being therefore astonished they came round the divine conjurer, and bestowing great praise on him, paid him the money which they had promised and went away.

SECOND STORY

OF THE PURCHASE OF THE HORSE'S EGG

After the Gooroo Noodle and his five disciples had arrived at the Matham, they went about relating the dilemma in which they had been placed in the river.

Upon this an old one-eyed woman, who was in the habit of sweeping the Matham, having heard in detail all that had happened, said, " I am of opinion that there was a mistake in the mode in which you counted yourselves and added up the sum. If one reckons, leaving out either himself or any other person, the amount will be erroneous; however, if another occasion should occur, I will tell you a method by which such a mistake as this may be avoided. Having picked up the ordure* which lies on the commons, collect it together, and when you have patted it smooth, gather around it, and stooping down, dip the ends of your noses in the dung. Then

---

* This is a suggestion which would not appear quite so extravagant to a Hindoo as it must to an European, for the women of an Indian family are frequently employed in collecting the ordure of cattle, which they form into flattened cakes and dry in the sun against rocks or walls. These cakes are used as fuel by all classes.

count the impressions made by your noses, and you may thus know, without any error in the account, how many persons there are. In this very same manner, some fifty or sixty years ago, did we take account of a number of women who were collected together."

They all replied, "This indeed is a capital plan and costs no money; it did not occur to any of us. Nevertheless, for all purposes, it will be best to buy a horse. Sir, you must by all means procure a horse." The Gooroo demanded how much the price of a horse would amount to. As they heard upon enquiry that it could not cost less than from fifty to a hundred pagodas, the Gooroo determined that he had not ability to pay so much.

The matter thus remained a good while under consideration, when one day they perceived that their milch cow, which had been turned out to feed, did not return home at the close of the evening; they sought her all over the village, but as, notwithstanding their search, she was not to be found, Blockhead on the following day went to seek her in the surrounding villages.

On his return to the Matham the third day, unable to discover her anywhere, he exclaimed with delight, "The cow, Sir, I cannot find: 'tis no matter, however, for I have met with a horse for us at a very low price." "How is that?" demanded the Gooroo with eagerness. To which Blockhead replied, "When I was on my return, after I had been searching from village to village, from common to common, from enclosure to enclosure, in order to find the milch cow, I perceived four or five mares grazing and reposing on the bank of a large lake. As I went on farther I found, in a place which was near, a number of horses' eggs hanging down in every direction, which could not be encompassed by one's two arms. Upon enquiry of one who came up, he informed me that they were in truth horses' eggs, and that the price of each of them was only four or five pagodas. Here is a fine opportunity, Sir. We can thus, at an easy rate, obtain a high-bred horse, and as for its docility, this will depend upon the manner in which we rear it and break it in." They all consented to this proposition, and having united Idiot with him, delivered into their hands five pagodas, and despatched them forthwith on their journey.

After Blockhead and Idiot had

set out, in the manner just mentioned, to purchase the horse's egg, Fool thus threw out a doubt. "Grant that the egg of a high-bred courser be obtained, still when obtained, it is only after having been sat upon that it will be hatched; but who in the world is to hatch it, I am sure I do not know. He says that it is not to be encompassed by one's two arms: though then we were to keep ten hens together upon it, they could not even stand upon it, much less cover it. Tell us then how we are to manage in this business." On hearing what he said, they all stared at each other with astonishment, and without opening their mouths, remained speechless. After a considerable pause, the Gooroo addressed himself separately to each of the three who were present, saying, "I see no other way but that one of us should sit on it." Upon this each made his excuses. "It is my business," says one, "to go daily to the river and fetch all the water that is wanted, as also to go to the jungle and procure canes for firewood; how therefore can I possibly hatch it?" Says another, "After remaining night and day without intermission in the kitchen, dressing rice, cooking all kinds of curries, making fancy cakes and boiling water, for everybody, thus killing myself at the stoves, how can the hatching be performed by me?" Says another, 'Before day-break I go to the river, and after having cleansed my teeth, rinsed my mouth, washed my face, purified my hands and feet, and completed all my ceremonies according to the rules, I have to go round the flower gardens, cull the new buds, bring them hither with due respect, tie long garlands, strew flowers over different idols, at the same time worshipping them, and daily assist at the Pooja of the deity. Such is my business; is it not?

With all this, how can I hatch it?"

To this the Gooroo replied, "This is all quite true; neither can it be accomplished by the other two who are gone away; for one of them has more business than he can finish, in making enquiries respecting those who come and go, in giving answers to the questions which they propose, and in hearing and settling the disputes which are brought before him. Finally, Blockhead, on all occasions when we wish to transact any business, is he not the person who goes to the shops, to the fairs and to the villages? It is very true, therefore, that you must follow those occupations which constantly require your attention. For my part, am I not here doing nothing? I will place the egg in my lap, embrace it with my arms, cover it with the skirt of my cloth, hug it in my bosom, guard it with tenderness, and thus hatch it. It is enough if we do but produce the horse, we will not regard the trouble which is to be endured."

Whilst all this deliberation was taking place in the Matham, Block-head and Idiot, who had set out in the third watch with the rising moon, after a journey of more than two kâdams and a half, bent their course towards the mark which they had before seen and noticed, and arrived at the borders of the lake where there was an abundance of pumpkins in fruit.

On perceiving this, being greatly delighted, they went to the countryman who was attending there and entreated him, saying, "Master, we earnestly conjure you to give us one of these eggs." He, in his turn, seeing their idiotism, said, "Hey-day! do you suppose yourselves fit to buy such high-bred horses' eggs as these? They are very costly indeed." To this they replied, "Go to Master, do we not know that five pagodas is the price of them? Look ye, friend, take your five pagodas and give us a good egg." To this he answered, "You are, to be sure, fine honest fellows. In consideration of your good qualities, I consent to give them to you at this price ; select therefore an egg to your liking, and go your ways, but do not publish it abroad that you have obtained it at this easy rate." They both of them selected and took away a fruit which was larger than all the rest, and rising early the next morning, they set out on their journey just as the day was breaking.

Blockhead having carefully

taken the egg and lifted it on his head, the other went before, shewing the way, and while they were thus going along, Blockhead began to say, "Ay, ay, our forefathers have said, *they who perform penance, are forwarding their own affairs.* We have now seen the proof of this with our own eyes. This in truth is the profit which has accrued by the penance continually performed by our Gooroo. A high-bred horse, which is worth a hundred or a hundred and fifty pagodas, we purchase and take to him for five." To which Idiot replied, "Needs this any reflection? Hast thou not heard the saying—*from* *pious actions* alone proceeds delight, all else is irrelevant and unworthy of praise.* From virtue, not only profit, but pleasure proceeds; except there be (virtue), all

---

* The Tamils reckon thirty-two kinds of pious actions, some of which are sufficiently fanciful : these comprehend, however, if not all the possible varieties of charitable works, at least more than most people perform. Their enumeration is as follows : 1. The building of hospitals for the poor. 2. Giving food to those whose employment is devotion. 3. Giving food to those who follow any of the six sects. 4. Supplying calendars or almanacs. 5. Furnishing remedies for the eyes. 6. Giving oil for the anointment of the head. 7. Associating with the female sex. 8. Marriage. 9. Sobriety. 10. Preserving the good works of another. 11. Raising a shed where water may be furnished gratis to passengers. 12. Building a house, either of rest for passengers, or for some religious devotee. 13. Building tanks and repairing roads. 14. Planting trees. 15. Planting groves for the convenience of travellers. 16. Giving food to animals. 17. Giving money to preserve the life of any living thing whatsoever. 18. Erecting posts for cows to rub themselves against. 19. Giving food to prisoners or slaves. 20. Giving boiled rice

else will be misery and disgrace. Did not my father for a long time practise many virtues ; and he found his profit and delight in the end, in having me born to him." To which the other replied, " Can this be doubted? *If you sow a castor-oil tree, will an ebony tree*

---

for sacrifices. 21. Causing to make sacrifices. 22. Giving garments. 23. Furnishing provisions for a journey. 24. Furnishing Brahmans with the means of bearing the expense of assuming the sacred thread. 25. Pouring milk into the sacrificial fire. 26. Making gifts, more especially of money. 27 Giving quick-lime to be eaten with betel leaf. 28. Paying for the barber employed in shaving another. 29. Furnishing remedies for diseases. 30. Giving drink to cows. 31. Furnishing a looking-glass. 32. Burning corpses. It would need a long commentary to explain the nature and value of these various good works. I confess myself unable to do so, but recommend that their merits should be made matter of conversation with the instructor, by those who study the Tamil language in India.

be produced? * From good actions, good will proceed, from evil actions, evil."

Thus conversing, after they had walked along for a considerable distance, the pumpkin, from striking against the bough of a tree which was bent and hanging down, was dashed out of his hands, and suddenly tumbling upon some shrubs which were spreading in bushes below, cracked and fell to pieces.

Upon this, a hare which was sitting in the bushes started up

---

* Perhaps it approaches still nearer to the very forcible interrogatory with which our Saviour inculcates the same moral: "Do men gather grapes of thorns or figs of thistles? Matt. vii. 16.

and ran away. Taking the alarm, they cried out, "Behold! the horse's foal which was in the shell has run away;" and followed after to catch and seize it. Running, regardless of hills or dales, or woods or commons, the clothes which they had on became entangled in the thorny bushes, and were partly torn and partly detained. They continued the pursuit, with their flesh lacerated by the stumps which they trod on, their blood flowing in consequence of the thorns which stuck into them, their bodies all streaming with perspiration, their hearts beating, their two ears closed, puffing and blowing with fatigue, and their bowels jolting; notwithstanding which, the hare was not caught, and they both fell down, wearied out and harassed with fatigue. In the meantime the hare went on, and becoming concealed, so as no longer to be kept in sight, it ran away to a great distance. They too, regardless of their weariness, rose up, and with legs limping and wounded by thorns, stones and stumps, searched in every direction. Journeying in this afflicted condition, they suffered hunger and fasting all that day, and after sunset arrived at the Matham.

When they entered in at the

gate, they smote their mouths, crying, "Alas! alas!" and beating themselves, fell down. "What is it? What is it? What harm has come to you?" demanded the rest; who came, and, taking them by the hand, raised them up. After the two had related in detail all the circumstances that had happened. Blockhead spoke as follows: "O Sir, since the day that I was born, I never beheld so swift a horse as this: of an ash colour, mixed with black; in form and size like a hare, and a cubit in length. Although a foal still in the nest, it pricked up its two ears, cocked its tail, which rose up the length of two fingers,* extended and stretched forth its four legs, and with its heart close to the ground, ran with a swiftness and impetuosity which can neither be expressed nor conceived."

Upon this, they were all bewailing, when the Gooroo appeasing them, said, "True indeed, the five pagodas are gone, but however, it is well that the horse's foal is gone also; if whilst a foal it runs in this manner, when hereafter it shall become full grown, who will be able to ride upon it? I truly am

---

* By "two fingers," is meant the breadth of two fingers, a finger's breadth being a measure in common use, and the word *length* applies to the tail.

an old man: a horse of this description, my friends, although it were presented to me gratis, I would not accept."

THIRD STORY

OF THE JOURNEY WHICH WAS MADE, MOUNTED ON AN HIRED OX

AFTER some time had elapsed, a necessity arose for performing a long journey. As they could not go so far on foot, they agreed for the hire of an ox without horns. They settled to give for its hire, three fanams a day, and after one watch from sunrise had been employed in various affairs, they set out upon their journey.

It being a terribly hot season,

as they travelled along, the rays of the sun darted directly upon them, and they found themselves in an open plain, without the advantage of a single tree or bush, and without either covering or shade. While they were thus jogging along, the old Gooroo, unable to endure the fierceness of the unrelenting heat, and bending like a green blade of corn, was in danger of falling off the ox. On perceiving this, his disciples laid hold of him and lifted him off, and, as there was no other shade, set him under the shadow of the ox, which they halted, and fanned him with their cloths. After he had by this means been much revived, as a cool breeze sprang up, he re-mounted the ox, and travelling gently along, they arrived, before the day declined, at a little village where they halted.

No sooner had they entered into a small rest-house there, than, on paying the ox-driver his three fanams, he asserted that it was not enough. "How is this," replied they, "is not this the daily hire that we originally agreed for with you?" To which he, objecting, vociferated, "It is true indeed, that for the accommodation of the ox, as a conveyance, this hire was agreed upon ; but, moreover, in the middle of the way, my ox afforded accommodation as an umbrella against the heat: must I not then have hire for this too?" They asserted that this was an imposition, and flying into a passion, opposed him and raised a great dispute. As the quarrel increased, all the villagers who were passing to and fro, both men and women, assembled and formed a crowd. In the meantime a Padeiyâchi,* who was the justice, having appeased the fray, heard the dispute on both sides, and demanded of them whether they would abide by the decision which he should pronounce, and the judgment which he should

* A certain caste of cultivators.

give: after which he spoke as follows:

"I* myself once travelling home, put up one night at a large caravanserai; where, besides lodging, they supplied, for money, those who frequented it with everything that might be wanted in the way of food. I, however, as I had not enough for my travelling expenses, said that I needed nothing. They then transfixed upon an iron spit a large leg of mutton, for those who had arrived that day, which they roasted by turning it over the burning coals. This continued

---

* This story, which, in other forms, is familiar to us in Europe, is derived from an oriental stock.

smoking with the heat, and the odour which it sent forth being very grateful, I thought that it would be nice to eat the bundleful of boiled rice, which I had brought, with this savoury smell, and begged permission to be allowed to turn the spit for a little while. Thus, holding the rice over the smoke, I turned the spit with one hand, whilst with the other I fed myself with gratification at the savoury odour. Afterwards, when I was thinking of going, the master of the caravanserai demanded payment for the odour which I had smelt. I asserted the injustice of his demand, and, both of us disputing together, we went before the headman of the village. Now he was a great Shastri, a very sensible man, extremely clever and much versed in the science of the law. Listen to the decision which he gave. 'For him who ate of the dish, the price is money, but for smelling the odour which issued from the dish, the price is the odour of money; this is my decision.' So saying, he called the master of the caravanserai near him, and forcing a bagful of money down upon his nose, he chaffed and scrubbed it. The other cried out, 'O dear! O dear! my nose is coming off, I have had sufficient payment.' Do ye hear this? Is not this justice, is not this law? This very decision applies to you. For journeying hither on the ox, the proper hire is money, and for remaining in the ox's shadow, the shadow of the hire-money is sufficient."

However, as the sun was now set, having settled the sound of the money, as the hire of the ox's shadow, he suddenly seized on the ox-driver, and having repeatedly thumped the money-bag upon his ear, he cried out, "Do'st hear?" To which he replied, "O yes, Sir, O yes, Sir, I have heard it, indeed I have heard it, my ear is sore; enough father, of hire enough." The Gooroo also said, "What I have already suffered sufficeth me; I cannot endure this vexation, take away thy ox; the remainder of the journey is short, in the morning I will proceed gently on foot." So saying, he discharged him. Then, greatly praising and complimenting the Justice who had so well settled his quarrel, he gave him his blessing and dismissed him.

FOURTH STORY

OF THROWING A FISH-HOOK TO CATCH THE HORSE

On the following day the Gooroo and his disciples dreading the heat, made ready as soon as the cock crew and set out on their journey. As they travelled at a slackened pace, before they had yet finished one kâdam, finding that the heat began to scorch them, they halted in a cool grove. Whilst they were refreshing themselves there, Dunce retired to the fields, and then went to wash his feet* in a neighbouring lake.

There was an Âyinar temple upon its bank, in which there was a large horse of newly baked clay, which had been brought and deposited there in fulfilment of a vow. The lake being full of water, and the water clear, Dunce saw the reflection of that clay horse in the lake ; and, astonished that a horse should stand in the water, as he perceived that it was of similar colour, size and appearance with the clay-horse which stood on the bank, there arose a suspicion with him that it

* This expression is equally guarded as the former, and has an implied meaning which cannot be mistaken.

might perhaps be its reflected image which appeared below.

Just* then, however, the water becoming undulated and ruffled by a breeze that blew over it, the horse also which appeared in it was agitated, and as he perceived that there was no motion whatever in the horse on the shore, he became convinced that the horse in the water was separate and alive; moreover, as if to drive it away, he shouted out, and pelted it with a stone. With this, the water becoming more undulated, the horse also seemed to him to raise his head, to

* This story reminds us of that told of the Wise Men of Gotham, who raked in a pond for the Moon.

kick out his feet, and to leap with his whole body in trepidation. So taking alarm, he ran to the rest and related everything that he had seen.

Upon this they all instantly arose and hastened to the spot, where, looking around them, they perceived the truth of what Dunce had reported. They afterwards consulted together how they should take it, but as none of them would consent to descend into the water and lay hold of it, after opposing and rejecting several modes which one and another suggested, they at length determined, that it would be the best plan, by casting a hook, in the same way as one would catch a fish, to catch this also, and thus draw it ashore.

They made preparations by taking as a hook, a sickle that one of them had with him, and this they baited with a bundle of boiled rice which they had brought, while for a line they took the turban that the Gooroo wore. In this manner, having thrust the sickle through the rice, they tied it with the turban, and threw it into the place where the horse made his appearance. By the great undulation of the water, from the impetus with which it plunged in, the horse also which appeared there, seemed as if seen to leap, to wriggle and to kick, in consequence of which they all took alarm and ran away. One of them, however, who had hold of the turban did not let it go, but remained with it in his grasp. After the waves of the lake had subsided, he drew softly near, and as he continued to troll the bundle of rice which had been cast in, some large fish in the lake bit at the cloth; perceiving signs of which he beckoned the rest to him by a signal with his hand and cried, "Look ye! the horse is biting the bait." On drawing up the turban after a little while, the cloth and the rice were both gone, in consequence of which, the sickle which was fastened to the turban stuck in a large weed that was spreading out beneath the water. They all cried out with delight, "Now that the hook has stuck in the horse's mouth, he is our own :" then uniting together they pulled at the turban, which, being an old one, gave way, and they all at the same instant fell on their backs.

A good man coming up at the moment when they had thus tumbled down, asked what was the matter, and they related everything as it had occurred. Upon this, he, perceiving their simplicity, veiled with a cloth the clay horse which was on the shore, and shewing them that the horse in the water was also thus hidden, he did away with the delusion.

They then pointed out the Gooroo, and related to the man, with every particular, how, from their not having money to purchase a horse, which was so absolutely necessary in consequence of his decrepit age, they had bought the egg of one; how it had been destroyed, and how they had suffered vexation on account of the hired ox. He, perceiving that they were well-meaning folks, and without guile, had pity on them, and said, "I have a lame horse, and old one indeed, however, it will be serviceable for journeys of the description you make ; fanam or kâsoo is unnecessary, I give it you gratis. Come all of you to my house." So saying, he took them away with him.

FIFTH STORY

OF GOING HOME ON HORSE-BACK

THAT good man carried them away in the manner already mentioned to the village where he lived, which was in the neighbourhood. He was not a rich man; he was indeed poor, but he was charitable; so he spread before them a supper, in which there was no lack of ghee, or milk, or tyer,* and gave them

* Milk curdled into a solid mass, by the addition of a small quantity of milk already curdled. It is usually eaten with rice.

betel leaf* and nut† and tobacco, and whatever else was requisite, in abundance.

On the following morning, he sent for the horse which was grazing in his fields, and setting it before the Gooroo presented it to him as a gift. The horse, besides being aged, was blind of an eye, shorn of an ear, lame in one of his fore legs, and limping in one of the hind legs: so that it was a conveyance suitable to the woeful form of the Gooroo. Although such his plight, they were all greatly delighted that they had got a horse,

* Piper Betel.

† Areca Catechu.

and that it had been obtained gratis. Gathering around, they lavished on it their caresses, this one patted it, that one laid hold of a leg and twisted it, one seized the tail and pulled it, another wiped its eyes, while another fed it by cramming grass into its mouth.

After this, on searching for the horse's trappings, he who had made them a present of the horse gave them an old saddle which was torn. However, as it wanted the hind-strap (crupper) which passes under the tail, they procured some pâlei-kodi stalks and tied them on: so likewise, as there was no rein to the bridle, they substituted twisted hay bands. After they had given themselves much trouble to obtain a belly band and girths, not being able to procure them, Blockhead went to a village in the neighbourhood, and purchased both these and a martingale.

When all the trappings had been thus obtained, the unlucky*

---

* If the 12th day of the Moon's age fall on a Sunday, the 11th on a Monday, the 5th on a Tuesday, the 2nd on a Wednesday, the 6th on a Thursday, the 8th on a Friday, the 9th on a Saturday, these days are accounted unlucky. On the contrary, if the 8th fall on a Sunday, the 9th on a Monday, the 6th on a Tuesday, the 3rd on a Wednesday, the 9th on a Thursday, the 13th on a Friday, the 14th on a Saturday, these days are esteemed lucky. In general, the 1st day of the moon's age, the 4th, the 6th, the 8th, the 9th, the 11th, the 12th, the 14th and the 15th, are esteemed unlucky, unless their ill-luck be corrected by the day of the week according to the above table. On the contrary, the 2nd, the 5th, the 7th, the 10th and the 13th, are esteemed lucky.

days were passed over, and at a fortunate moment, according to the rules of astrology, all the village having come forth in company with them, shouting out and cheering, they placed the Gooroo Noodle on horse-back at the head of the procession. Then, one of the five disciples laying hold of the bridle pulled forward. One placed near the tail, hooted, and drove the beast on. Two of them at the two sides, keeping hold of the Gooroo's legs, supported him; while another in front, acting as herald, cried, "Take ye care, take ye care, look out, look out;" and thus they went along.

After they had travelled merrily along for a considerable distance, the collector of toll belonging to the highway came running up, and stopping them, demanded five fanams for the horse. To this they replied, by crying out, " What! toll for a horse ridden by a Gooroo! Has this anything to do with commerce? This forsooth is a horse given by a person out of charity, who perceived that owing to his decrepit age he was unable to go on foot: what toll is there for this? 'Tis an injustice." As he would not quit his arrest, even until it was high noon, seeing no other way, they gave the five fanams. The

Gooroo, too, reflecting that if he had been without a horse, this vexation would not have been occasioned, was in great tribulation.

They went to refresh themselves in a choultry which was near, and to a good man whom he found there, the Gooroo himself began making great complaint. "I never," said he, "mounted a horse from the day that I was born. Now to-day, on the occasion of my riding for the first time, this is the injustice which I have experienced. Shall the money, which they thus wickedly obtain, like thieves who unlawfully take possession of the road, do them any good? Shall not the money, which they consume my belly by receiving, become a fire to them ?" To which the other replied, "This, Sir, is the temper of the times ; in these days, money is the Gooroo, money is the deity ; we have heard it said of old, that *if you but name money, even a corpse will open its mouth.* Now-a-days, Sir, there is no other care or love but money." The Gooroo answered, "In these times there are some, who if they see money, though it be in ordure, will not scruple to lick it out." Said the other, "Is there any doubt of this ? And even that, Sir, doth not stink to them : listen to an evidence of this.

"A certain king, * from a desire of money, after he had imposed upon his kingdom all sorts of taxes which had not existed before, levied a tax also upon urine. This, even his own son not enduring, he remonstrated with his father, saying that it was shameful to demand such a stinking tax. The king, however, dismissed his son without making a reply. After many days had elapsed, and the money had been collected for the tax which had been imposed, the king, sending for his son, desired him to smell that money: 'Does it stink?' demanded

* This is the well known story of Vespasian and Titus, which the Author has artfully introduced in illustration of his subject.

he. The son, not thinking of any ulterior meaning, said it smelt well enough; upon which the king replied, 'This is the very money from the urine tax.' Dost hear me? It is enough, if the money but comes; it is no matter, Sir, how it comes."

After they had in this manner passed the day in much conversation, in the evening the Gooroo again mounted the horse, and when they had travelled along they halted in a hamlet. They did not tether the horse, but turned him out to feed at night, and when they went in the morning to seek him for their journey, he was not to be found. On entering and searching from house to house, a person had detained him tied up in his enclosure, and when they requested that he would give him up, he replied, "The whole thirty hours of the night he has been feeding on my grain, by which, as I have suffered much injury, I will positively not let him go." Upon this the chief of the village went himself to him; but although he endeavoured to appease him, both by entreaties and threats, he said that he would agree to give him up, only on condition that the damage should be made good. A number of persons assembled, who having enquired into the injury which had been done by the grazing, and having estimated what had been trodden down and what had been fed off, pronounced that there was a damage of ten fanams, or, at least, that there was a damage of eight fanams. In the end, however, an agreement was made for four fanams; which the man having received, gave up the horse.

As for the Gooroo, being greatly distressed, "Wherefore have I this horse?" said he, "how many expenses, how many sorrows, how many degradations have been incurred in consequence of its coming; all this, my friends, is ill-befitting my dignity." So saying, he resolved firmly to go on foot. Upon this, both his disciples and the village folk cried, "Fie, fie, this ill-beseems you, besides, you are unable to walk on foot." Then a certain Valloovan hearing all this, said, "You need not grieve, Sir. Undoubtedly all these calamities have come upon you, from the sin which has possessed the horse. If you, once for all, will incur an expense and give me five fanams, I will cast out and remove that sin." Reflecting, that "*if one fears expense, business cannot be done,*" they consented to give the money, and told him to cast out the sin.

Then the Valloovan, in order to deceive them, performed several ceremonies, plucked some green leaves, sprinkled them over the horse, screamed out, " Moona! moona! ah! oh!" And having performed circumgyrations round him, he came thrice to the right, and after patting and stroking the horse from the tail to the head, seized hold of the single ear. " In this very ear," said he, " all the sin is lodged. It was in order to cast out such a sin as this, that the other ear was heretofore cut off. Now, if we cut off this also, the sin of the present day will be suppressed and stayed." With this, having sharpened a chopper, they cut off the ear, and in a trice bore it to a distance, in order that the sin might not attach to any one. They then dug a deep pit, buried it, and covering it with earth, placed a mark there and came away. As all that day was consumed, on the following morning they departed, and after having suffered much trouble arrived at the Matham.

SIXTH STORY

OF THE BRAHMAN'S PROPHECY

After their arrival at the convent, the Gooroo was very much out of spirits. The gift-horse was a very defective horse, yet it was a great happiness to him that it had come without purchase ; still, however, harping and harping upon the sorrows and misfortunes which had happened on the road on account of the horse, he continued to suffer great anxiety of mind : so, assembling his disciples, he began to give them divers sage counsels. " Brethren, I perceive every day more and more, that all the pleasures of the world are false pleasures. Good unmixed with evil, a sweet unmixed with bitter, and joy unmixed with sorrow, are here unattainable. Alas ! alas ! were we not greatly delighted, that, through civility, we had obtained a horse without paying for him ? Ye have witnessed the sad misfortunes which visited us, and, on that very day, immediately followed this good fortune. Must we swallow so much bitterness, in licking up one drop of honey ? Ah ! even the grain of fine rice is within its husk, and to fruits of every kind there is a skin and a stone. All this is indeed true ; nevertheless, the evil which I have endured within the space of one day is extreme. It is certainly not befitting me to go about riding on horseback. Shall I have the audacity to go in opposition to the destiny above? No, no. It will be proper, then, hereafter to send the horse back again." To this all the disciples with one accord replied, "This must not be ; this must not be. Do not talk so, Sir. Is this a horse which you have purchased? Is this a horse which we have sought? No indeed, it is a horse which came of itself, as a providential assistance; did it not? If we send it back, it will be to go in opposition to the divine will; will this be proper? This will, indeed, be a sin, Sir. Besides this, there is nothing to excite alarm, now that that Valloovan has cast out the sin which had got possession of the horse."

By their stating at large, this, as well as many other reasons, the Gooroo himself having recovered his spirits, said, "Be it according as you have said; however, in order that the mishap which we met with the other day, may not occur in future, it will not do to turn the horse out to feed at night, but we must positively keep him tied up in-doors, and I do not know of any place for that purpose." Then, said Simpleton "What need of consideration for this? I will go now directly and cut some Banian branches, and bring them, and in a moment I will construct a neat stable up in the corner."

The instant that he spoke, he set out, and ascending a large spreading Banian tree which was by the road side, he began to cut* with an axe a straight branch which

---

* This adventure will remind the reader of that admirable stroke of satire in Hogarth's engraving of an Election: where a foolish fellow sits at the extremity of the Crown sign-post, and saws the portion

projected. He, however, stood at the end, and chopped the part next the trunk; which a Brahman traveller who was coming along the road having perceived, cried out, "Ho! brother, do not stand in this manner, you yourself will fall together with the branch." To this he replied, "Comest thou with this evil boding to me?" With that he hurled at the Brahman a knife which he kept sheathed at his waist. Whilst the other thinking, "Let this fool learn by suffering," retreated and made his escape.

---

on which he is supported. Our Author wrote before Hogarth's time, but the idea is very ancient; for, as I learn from an eminent Sanskrit scholar, it is contained in an anecdote related of Kâlidâsa.

As for Simpleton, he chopped away, still standing in the same manner in which he had stood before, so that when the wood was more than half cut through, it broke, and he himself fell down with it. "Am! am! ma! exclaimed he, "that Brahman is a great Shâstri, a mighty Prophet, it has happened just as he predicted." So saying, he quickly rose up, and ran to overtake the Brahman. This latter, perceiving him running all on a sudden towards him, stood in terror, doubting what this senseless wild beast might do. Simpleton, approaching, made him a reverence, and said, "Sir, you are a great

Shâstri, pray prophesy for me yet once more; I am a disciple of the Gooroo Noodle, for whom I have a great affection. As he is of a decrepit age, I am fearful that he will die in the course of a short time. Do pray now, for my comfort, tell me at what period his end will be, and what will be the signs that will appear previously to it."

The Brahman, in order to effect his escape, made various excuses; but, as the other would not quit him, he at last said, "*Âsanam shîtam jîvana nâsham.*" "What is this, Sir? pray tell me its meaning," asked the other importunately. The Brahman replied, "On whatsoever day your Gooroo's posteriors shall become cold, it will be a sign that his death is at hand."

So Simpleton, having made obeisance, departed, and dragging the branch which he had cut to the Matham, related circumstantially all the particulars that had passed. The Gooroo upon this was very sorrowful, and thus spoke. "It cannot be asserted that the said Brahman is not a great Shâstri, for everything immediately happened to thee, exactly as he had foretold. In like manner, the prophecy which he has pronounced and sent to me, must be infallible. *Âsanam shîtam jîvana nâsham*, is a true saying. For the future, great care will be requisite : my feet must never be washed, and for the rest—God's will be done."

SEVENTH STORY

OF FALLING OFF THE HORSE

After the circumspection, which has been mentioned, had been for some time used, they set out upon a tour from village to village ; impelled by the consideration, that, should they travel around the district, the disciples might collect their money, but that in the Matham no income could be realized.

One day, when they were on their return to the Matham, as the Gooroo was jogging along on horseback, his turban happened to fall off behind him, in consequence of encountering the branch of a tree which hung downwards.* Thinking that the disciples had picked it up, after he had travelled on quietly for a considerable distance, he asked them, "Where is my turban? please to give it me." They replied, "It is yonder, and probably lies on the spot where it fell." Upon which he grew angry, and said, "Is it not necessary to pick

---

* The roads, in India, are not infrequently lined with Banian trees, whose wide-spreading boughs, covered with thick foliage, afford a welcome shade to the traveller. From these boughs, the largest and lowest of which are horizontal, numerous roots are suspended, which in time reach the ground and become new trunks. They may with truth be said to hang downwards; an expression, which would scarcely apply to the bough of any other tree.

up everything that hath fallen ?" So Idiot immediately ran off, and as he was bringing along the fallen turban which he had picked up, he placed in it some dung loosely evacuated by the horse (for he had been feeding on the commons upon grass that was green, in consequence of some showers of rain which had fallen that night), and delivered it into the Gooroo's hand.

He then became exceedingly enraged, crying out, "Fie, fie!" To this they all, with one accord, replied, "How is this, Sir? Did you not deliver your instructions before, saying that everything which fell was to be picked up; and now, because

Idiot acts according to those instructions, you fly into a passion ; wherefore is this ?" As for the Gooroo, he replied, " Not so. There are some things which it is proper to pick up, and others which it is improper to pick up. You should act with some shew of sagacity." To this they replied, " We are not men so clever as all that." So they requested that he would write down, separately, such things only as they were required to pick up, and these he wrote accordingly.

After this, in travelling along, the ground being slippery and wet, the lame horse, which tottered as it went, tripped and fell down, and the Gooroo tumbling head downwards and feet upwards into a large hole which was near, roared out for help, and cried, " Pray run and pick me out." The disciples ran to him, and one of them taking out the cadjan,* which he had before written and given to them, began to read thus : " To pick up a fallen turban†—to pick up a fallen waist-cloth and short cloth—to pick up

---

* A name, probably of Portuguese origin, used by Europeans at Madras to signify the leaf of the Palmyra tree. The languages of Southern India are usually written, or rather engraved, on this material.

† The articles of clothing among the Tamuls are few and simple ; though their names, some of which are synonymous, and others expressive of differences in manufacture, colour and other circumstances, are extremely numerous. It seems probable that, anciently, they wore no sewn garments, and that the jackets now so much in use among the higher classes of

a fallen jacket and drawers." Thus the Gooroo lay there naked, while they went over each article, one by one, according as it was read out, and notwithstanding all his entreaty

---

citizens, and the bodices worn by dancing women, as well as females of the higher orders, were introduced by the Mussulmans on their conquest of the country. To this day, those who, residing far from towns, and following rural occupations, are less disturbed in their observance of the customs of their ancestors, wear none but long unsewn cloths, in the precise state in which they come from the loom ; and in none of the Ancient Sculptures of Southern India, are either jackets or bodices to be found, the men or gods being represented naked, and the women being furnished with a broad ornamented belt, which passes horizontally across the breasts and under the arms. The turban is likewise of modern introduction and partial use ; Brahmans, with the exception of those who hold official situations, seldom wear it, and many other classes, more especially in the country, go bare-headed even in the hottest weather. The genuine dress of the men, therefore, consists of a cloth which delicacy absolutely demands, and which is the only covering worn by the labouring classes—a cloth of 8 cubits in length, which is passed several times

and all his rage, because this was not written in the cadjan, they persevered in refusal, saying, "Sir, where is it written that you are to be picked up? shew us. We will do exactly according to what is

---

around the waist and between the legs, thus entirely covering the lower half of the person—a cloth, of 4 four cubits length, which is usually carried over one of the shoulders and is occasionally used to cover the head—a cloth, of from 19 to 20 cubits, which envelops the upper part of the person. Perhaps the sort of short trousers reaching half way down the thigh, and worn by soldiers and athletæ, may be also of ancient origin. To these we may annex the modern additions, of the turban, of 30 cubits length—linen vest, which fits the body in the upper part and has a full skirt, and the trousers worn by dancers.

The true dress of the women is a single cloth of 14 cubits in length, called by dexterity in the art of wrapping this around the waist, and bringing the end over the shoulder, the females in India form as elegant and modest a dress as that made with so much labour, and adjusted with so much art, by the fair sex in Europe. The use of the needle and scissors, therefore, which some seem so anxious at the present time to teach them, would prove at best but a needless art.

written ; but we will never consent to do that which is not written." He, perceiving their obstinacy and seeing no other way of escape, took a cadjan and a stile, and wrote, in the place where he was lying, "And if I fall you are to pick me up."

His disciples, when they saw what was written, all, with one accord, went and picked him up. As his body was entirely covered with mud, because there was muck in the hollow into which he had fallen, they washed him in some water which was at hand ; and, afterwards, having put on all his clothes as before, they seated him on the horse and conveyed him to the Matham.

EIGHTH STORY

OF THE INTERMENT OF THE GOOROO

From the great alarm and bustle, on the occasion when he fell and lay in the hole, no one called to mind the prophecy which the Brahman had previously made. It was only after having again mounted on horseback, that the Gooroo himself, perceiving that his posteriors were cold, grew sorrowful. Nevertheless, he refrained from saying anything, until their arrival at the Matham.

Owing to the shock of falling at his decrepit age, he could obtain no sleep that night, but tossed about restlessly, and suffered great tribulation from the thoughts of the above-mentioned prophecy. Not allowing himself to suppose, that the pain which agitated his frame and caused his restlessness, arose from the fall from the horse into the pit; he was confirmed in the notion, that it doubtless all proceeded from his approaching death, occasioned by the coldness of his rump. With this thought he was distracted and terrified within himself during the whole night, and unable to close his eyes even for a single instant, he groaned frequently, and, urged by the unsettled state of his mind, he afterwards at break of day sent for his disciples.

On their coming to see him, they were greatly alarmed to perceive, that his countenance was changed; that his two eyes had sunk in their sockets; that his face was withered and shrivelled, and that over it there was a pale hue mixed with brown; that his mouth was without moisture; his speech confused, and that he stared as it were upon vacancy. Then, fetching a deep groan, he exclaimed, "O! my brethren, place me in the sepulchre and perform the rites of burial to my corps." "How is that, Sir?" demanded they in terror. "How is that!" replied the Gooroo, "have ye then forgotten the words, *Âsanam shîtam jîvana nâsham.* In the pit, into which I fell yesterday, there was much water and mud, in consequence of which my rump became wet. Nevertheless, owing to the mishap which then took place, this did not occur to me. I afterwards perceived that my posteriors were very cold, and I thought upon the Shastra which the Brahman had pronounced. Accordingly, I have experienced pain of body and uneasiness during the whole night, nor have I obtained the least sleep, so that I am become fully sensible that my death is approaching. Further deliberation is needless, ye will speedily prepare for my interment."

They, too, on thinking of that augury, were terrified ; but although terrified, they did not disclose, but suppressed, their inward alarm, and administered every species of consolation in order to tranquillize the Gooroo's mind. Preceiving that, notwithstanding all that they could say, the tribulation of his mind was not appeased, they sent for one named Asangadan (the mocker), the son of Achedanamoorti (the irrational), who had formerly been the soothsayer of the village, and took him to cast out the evil spirit which possessed their Gooroo, and to comfort his mind. After he had heard all the circumstances which had previously occurred, Asangadan came, and, with eyes, mouth and nose, convulsed (by his grimaces), demanded, "What is the matter with you, Sir? Say, what ailment has come upon you, what pain, what grief, what affliction? My Gooroo! my Master! my Father!" To all this, the Gooroo made no other answer, except the sentence, *Âsanam shîtam jîvana nâsham*. Then the other replied, "Very well then, that Brahman has asserted, forsooth, that a coldness of your rump will be your destruction, and I will cause the heat of his rump to be his destruction. Point me out that Brahman, I will perform rice-beater Pôôja upon him, and thus cast out and put an end to all the evil which has happened through his means. Point him out immediately, point him out."

"Is there," said the Gooroo, "such a pôôja, as rice-beater pôôja? I have never seen or heard of such a pôôja; tell me what it is." To this, Asangadan began to reply, saying, "This sort of pôôja is certainly a pôôja which is not to be found among the

Oodsameiyams, or Poorrachchameiyans. Listen attentively.

"There was a merchant who was a great worshipper of Shivan; and who, from his desire to give food daily to Pandârams, used to invite them to a meal wherever he met them. He had no children, and as for the wife whom he had married, it being a great plague to her to dress and serve rice in this manner daily for one or two Pandârams, her husband's way of going on was by no means agreeable to her; nevertheless, as she knew that if she said anything to her husband on this subject he would not brook it, she hit upon a stratagem. One day, the merchant being in the bazar, he called a Pandâram whom he met and said to him, 'Sir, I mean to distribute alms in my house to-day;' and, as the other accepted the invitation, he added, 'I am busy in the bazar just now; do you yourself go to my house, give notice to my wife, and wait until I arrive.' The Pandâram went away blithely, and delivered the merchant's message to his wife. To this she, perceiving that he was one who had never been there before, replied, 'Very well; please, Sir, to remain here.' So saying, she spread a mat upon the bench of the house. She then immediately proceeded to sweep the court thoroughly, sprinkled it everywhere with cow dung, purified her feet and hands, and then with much solemnity took in her hands the beater* for pounding rice. She

---

* To deprive the rice of its husk, which is a domestic office assigned to the females of the family, a long pestle or rather staff, made of ebony or some other heavy wood, and shod with iron, is employed. The rice called, when in the husk, *Paddy* is collected into a heap upon a hardened floor, or sometimes in a hollow in the ground, and two women usually work together. They stand opposite to one another with the heap between them, and each receives and raises the instrument with the left hand, and then forces it down again violently with the right, giving it a slight inclination forwards, so that it may easily be caught by the left hand of the opposite party. As the rice becomes dispersed, it is pushed back into the centre with their left feet, causing a side movement; whence results a constant, though slow, revolution around the heap. This work, as indeed every other kind in India, which is performed by more than one person, and admits of adaptation to musical measure, is accompanied by a song.

then rubbed it all over with ashes, and having smeared herself also, laid the rice-beater in the middle of the court, and prostrating herself three times before it, muttered some incantations. When she had pronounced these, she wiped the rice-beater again, and placed it

---

From a consideration of the above custom, it seems to me not unlikely, that the operation referred to in the following passage of the Proverbs, ch. xxvii. 22, may have been that of clearing grain of the outer husk, and not that of pounding it into flour : "Though thou shouldest bray a fool in a mortar, among wheat with a pestle, yet will not his foolishness depart from him." Which may mean, "Though you should endeavour to separate him from his follies, as you separate wheat from its husk, by pounding, you would not succeed." This explanation seems the more probable, from the frequent allusion throughout the Scriptures to grinding wheat in mills, which were undoubtedly of the same kind as the hand-mills used in India. *Vide* Exod. xi. 5, Judges xvi. 21, Matt. xxiv. 41, Isa. xlvii. 2.

where it had been before. The Pandâram, who had been watching all this, was greatly astonished, and said, 'I have now witnessed wonders which I never to this day beheld. Pray, Dame, what sort of pôôja is this?' To this she replied, 'This is a kind of pôôja peculiar to the deity of our caste. You will hereafter understand it well,' she added, as she was entering the house, in a low tone, as if talking to herself, 'it will be completed on your head.' Although she thus spoke, yet just as she intended, it caught the Pandâram's ear. 'Have I not providentially escaped with my life,' thought he :

so, as soon as the merchant-woman had entered into the house, without making a noise, he effected his escape. No sooner was he gone, than the merchant came, 'Where, hussey, is the Pandâram whom I sent?' demanded he. She replied, 'He is a pretty Pandâram—is he not?—whom you have sent this time. As soon as he arrived he asked me to give him the rice-beater; to which I replied, the merchant will be here immediately, I must not give it you without his permission; stay a little. So saying, behold how I spread the mat for him; but he, without listening to me, instantly broke away.' The merchant answered, 'Not so, hussey, whatever Pandârams may ask, you have my consent to give them.' So saying he took the rice-beater in his hand, and went out in the street to seek the Pandâram and give it him. The Pandâram, in order to see the end of the affair which was about to happen, remained crouched in an alley in the street, and when he spied the merchant coming with his rice-beater, 'See, see, he is coming to close the pôôja upon my head,' thought he, and so he took to his heels. The merchant, too, ran in pursuit of him, crying out, 'Pandâram, Pandâram,' while he increased his speed more and more; till, in the end, the merchant, unable to run any longer in consequence of being advanced in age, and having a pot belly, returned to his own house. Such is rice-beater pôôja, and destruction will no more come upon you, Sir, than will the Brahman's posteriors become heated, if I accomplish it upon his back."

Upon this the Gooroo Noodle laughed, and said, "It is with reason that they call you Asangadan (the mocker), for you are always cracking your jokes." The other perceiving that the Gooroo laughed, left off banter and again took up the discourse. "Sir, the words which the Brahman spoke are according to truth, indeed; but it is necessary to understand the meaning of them rightly. True it is, that if a coldness be perceived in the posteriors, it is a sign of death; but it will be, as he asserted, only when the rump grows cold without any extraneous cause. You fell into water and mire: if upon this your posteriors became cold, is it any great wonder? It would in that case be a wonder if they did not grow cold. Now, therefore, abandon this chagrin. For the future, if, without sitting down in mire, or falling into the water, or without any other extraneous cause, you perceive the *Âsanam shîtam,* then you may infer that the *jîvana nâsham* is nigh at hand. Except in so far, all else, Sir, is nonsense." What Asangadan said, penetrated into the Gooroo's mind, and it appeared to him like reason; therefore, having brightened up a little, he arose, and began to eat, and to talk, and to go about from place to place.

After but a very few days had in this manner passed, one night, during his sleep, there fell incessantly a heavy shower of rain. In consequence of this, a dripping of water from the roof fell upon the Gooroo's bed, directly close to his posteriors; notwithstanding which, it was unknown to him from his being asleep. After the rain, and with it the dripping, had ceased, the Gooroo having rolled in his sleep, lay slumbering with his rump immediately upon the wet which had fallen. By the coldness thus produced, he suddenly awoke; and perceiving that his rump was exceedingly cold, he became convinced that now there was no extraneous cause whatever to produce the cold, and that the period of his death was arrived.

The disciples, also, without perceiving any external origin for the coldness, supposed that even the coldness of the bed proceeded from the frigidity of the Gooroo's rump, and thought, therefore, that this was the time of the fulfilment of the Prophecy. The people of his caste, also, who came to visit him, as they were possessed of about as much sense as themselves, coincided in all that was said; while the Gooroo uttered no other answer to those who came, but, "Now, without failure, *Âsanam shîtam jîvana nâsham.*"

Unable to sustain the increased depression of spirits, and the diminution of bodily strength, which in this manner he suffered from day to day, he one day fell into a swoon. Upon this they all made lamentation; and, placing their hands upon their heads,* began to weep and to howl, crying out, "Alas! alas! he is deceased, he is dead!" And, after performing the ceremonies appertaining to burial, they proceeded to bathe him.

For this purpose, having filled brimful of water a large trough which was in the Matham, they tossed the supposed corpse into it, and having pressed him down, a number of them with one accord

---

* This method of shewing affliction was customary among the Jews: thus, "And Tamar put ashes on her head, and rent her garment of divers colours that was on her, and *laid her hand on her head*, and went on crying." 2 Sam. xiii. 19. See also Jerem. ii. 37.

began to rub and to wash him. When thus washed, he recovered from the swoon ; but being unable to draw breath in the water, and incapable of making any signs with his hands and feet, which they squeezed together, the Gooroo Noodle perished, through their stupidity, by the hands of these idiots.

Upon this, a great multitude having assembled, they placed him in a sitting posture in a litter adorned with flowers, and raising him up, they crowded together before, behind, and at the sides. Whilst his disciples came and carried him along, chanting thus,

Âsanam shîtam jîvana nâsham ; and, having placed him in the grave, they buried him.